METAMORPHOSIS:

AN ANTHOLOGY OF WRITING FROM ABERYSTWYTH UNIVERSITY'S CREATIVE WRITING MA

The Aberystwyth University Creative Writing MA course sees students engage in workshops, critical and creative discussions, and preparation for future careers in the literary field. This anthology was curated, edited, and launched by students completing their Master's in 2024 as an optional component of their 'Writer as Professional' module. The contributors to the anthology include current and past MA students, as well as Creative Writing Undergraduates. For many of those included, this is their first opportunity to be published.

ISBN: 978-1-916938-92-2

The authors have asserted their right to be identified as the authors of this Work in accordance with the Copyright, Designs and Patents Act 1988

Cover designed by Aaron Kent

Edited by Robin Luffman, Laura Janosik, Louise Rowland, and Alison Ehringer

Typeset by Aaron Kent

Broken Sleep Books Ltd
PO BOX 102
Llandysul
SA44 9BG

Metamorphosis

Edited by
Robin Luffman, Laura Janosik,
Louise Rowland, and Alison Ehringer

Broken Sleep University Press

Contents

INTRODUCTION

Many themes were considered for this anthology, but from my shaky recollection of being sat around a classroom of the Hugh Owen building while not-yet-angry wasps worked on their nest outside, 'Metamorphosis' was the only one that got immediate and unanimous approval. I think this was for a few reasons. The first and most obvious was that we were all looking towards the end of our time at Aberystwyth, which – for some of us – has been four years of our lives. Chris Ward's poem 'What Comes Next' (23) and Alice Leroy's prose 'Home' (74) really capture that distinctly-university sense of growing into yourself in a place that Chris calls 'not quite home, but home enough.' These years have been framed by the idea of maintaining a connection to a far-away place while moving further and further away from the people we were there.

That isn't to say all of the work collected here explores change at a distance, many of the works invite us inside the home. We owe it to the diversity in style, experience, and perspective of our contributors to show us how those familiar four walls can change us through so many different eyes. We see a time capsule to the best and worst times in Lara Schaele's 'Versions of Myself' (14) and Blue Stareng's 'The Bedroom' (61); we see safety in Freya Blyth's 'Recovering After Breakdown' (13); we see homes as sanctuaries for clandestine relationships in Bec Lang's 'Up in the Heavens' (33), and as memorials to lost ones in Louise Rowland's 'The Toothbrush' (68); if we allow ourselves to wander out to the back garden, we may even find fertile ground where we can grow our own suspiciously-alive 'Sprouts' (46).

Our authors also showcased the metamorphosis of bodies, whether that be the intimate exploration of Rakyah Assam's 'O!' (6), the disruption of Robyn Pringle's art (55), seizing control of the body's changes in Fresno Thomas' 'diy' (17), or laying it to rest in A. J. Sharpe's 'Necrobiome Love Affair' (7). All this on top of the shifting memories of Alison Ehringer's 'Tyranny of Time' (22) and Rose Gifford's 'Stop Motion' (10), and the equally shifting environments of Laura Janosik's 'Per Aspera' (29) and Gracie Eland's 'Moon Child' (56).

At every step of the way with this anthology, the sheer amount of support, enthusiasm, and completely original takes on our theme have really and truly blown me away and proved that the culture of creativity in Aberystwyth is only growing stronger. Those works I haven't mentioned here weren't left out for any reason other than the art, poetry, and prose the theme 'metamorphosis' spawned were so varied it would be impossible and reductive to categorise them all. As it turns out, change is one of life's constants and it truly pervades everything, from the widest ocean to the farthest reaches of the galaxy and home again. So, I've left them as fun surprises (enjoy!).

The only thing left to say is a massive thanks to the Imaginary Homelands project, Aberystwyth's Centre for Creative Wellbeing, and Broken Sleep Books, without whom this project would look very, very different. We're endlessly grateful for all the support of the English and Creative Writing department, but particular thanks from all of us go to Dr Naji Bakhti and Dr Jacqueline Yallop, who are (in our academic opinion) legends.

Lastly, thanks to everyone who contributed and you, for buying this! A portion of the money raised from the sale of the MA Anthology goes to AberAid, a fantastic local refugee charity.

Although it is for a good cause, I do really hope everyone enjoys these collected creative works as much as we all have, I could not be any prouder to be a part of bringing them all together.

By the way, we're all leaving this year, so that wasps' nest outside the Hugh Owen classroom is someone else's problem. Good luck!

— Robin Luffman, Editor-in-Chief

O!

In my worst dreams I am rendered
into my constituent parts.
I approach myself from the outside:
a short and dark island
of milk and blood
littered with fingernail and fragment
of calcified stone
my hours alphabetised
in unvisited archives
in damp infested library basements.
All my words and efforts
reduced to moving wind,
a mere gasp
collecting friction as it rolls against
the ground and bushes,
the sound measuring the spaces between walls.
It slips through.
A deep moan
with no burden of meaning.

NECROBIOME LOVE AFFAIR

I look as though I were asleep.

The soft summer breeze whispers a soothing lullaby through meadow grass as I lay, tucked away, hidden by the undulating waves of green. I stare up at the bright blue sky with glassy eyes, the sun shining down upon my cold corpse — its warmth is wasted on the dead. Gravity pulls my blood towards the cool, damp earth, pooling it beneath my skin. I am turning into stone already, petrifying as rigor mortis sets in, limbs stiffening and muscles locking into place.

Nobody has found me yet; I am alone.

Forgotten.

But not by the flies.

Their wings whine loudly as they flutter down towards me, attracted to me — to death. I latch onto the noise, let it drown out the crushing solitude.

Their small green bodies gleam golden in the sun, dozens of glittering jewels creeping across my corpse. Crawling towards my orifices, they rub their little fly legs together lustily as they lay clusters of hundreds of ivory eggs. They buzz inside of my nostrils and scrabble into my ear, filling me with potential. They love me.

My soul smiles: I am not really alone.

We are changing together.

My stomach bloats as gas builds inside, my skin becoming taut like a drum. My abdomen is tinted green, the colour blooming out from the right side of my body; the rest is marbled, vivid oranges and yellows flowering across my skin. My skin blisters and slips. A foul smell emanates from me.

I am teeming with life.

The maggots have hatched. Their pale beige bodies writhe and wriggle in masses inside of me hungrily: luxuriating in the gore, celebrating my corpse, worshipping the feast that I am. With tiny, hooked mouths they tear into the soft decaying tissue, ripping me apart and devouring me.

As they eat, they moult — discarding the old and embracing the new, growing bigger every time.

I am not alone.

We are changing together.

The smell worsens, getting stronger as fluids drain out of me, a dark puddle pooling out and seeping into the soil beneath me. My body breaks down, my skin sinking into the recesses of my skeleton as I collapse inwards. My bones jut out, every rib and joint visible beneath the black leathery sheet my skin has become.

I stare at the sunny summer sky above me as wispy white clouds float serenely across it; my lips are gone, my teeth bared into a distorted grin.

The maggots abandon my body, slipping away into the soil.

I am alone.

Aren't we changing together?

I am a husk.

My flesh continues to disappear as my body dries out. The smell changes, becomes cheesy. Fermentation takes hold, mould spreading from my body and creeping across the ground.

New insects come — beetles that tear at my ligaments, gorging themselves on my toughened skin, laying their own eggs now.

Maybe this is all I am good for.

The maggots emerge from their pupation, flies now. I wait for them to bury into me again, start the cycle anew — but they leave, uncaring. I am an empty vessel with no soft flesh left to feast upon. Useless to them, a waste of their time. Ugly.

Love is not blind.

I feel alone.

I have changed too much for their liking.

My bones, bleached white from the sun, lay forgotten in the meadow. Wildflowers spring up from where my skeleton lays — blue cornflowers, yellow poppies, and pink primroses, thriving on the nitrogen-rich dirt.

There is a buzzing — not flies, but bees this time, their nectar-drunk bodies dancing between the petals. My soul flutters, hopeful.

I got you flowers. Please stay.

I don't want to be alone.

CHANGE IS TIRING

STOP MOTION

It is the first day of spring. Tart blackberries are beginning to ripen and bloody the evergreen and there is a light chill in the air, nipping like an old dog with no teeth. Christopher makes his way to the kitchen, careful not to wake his mum. He pulls his waders up to his knees and unlatches the back door, leaving it ajar; there is no one around for miles.

The first nest of dipper chicks to ring is at the glade edge, just over the hill, beneath a bridge that arches over the river Teme like an open mouth. He has been going there as long as he could walk — to swim, to monitor the chicks with his dad and, once, to stow an egg in his pocket. He hid it under his bed, periodically taking it out. He was transfixed by the pure white dome of it, exotic as a shark tooth, smoothed by the rough fingers of the river like quartz, desperate for it to hatch.

Instead, it degenerated, becoming translucent like a cataract eye. After a month, he slung it from his window, heavy with guilt at having tampered with something he couldn't fix.

Dippers are difficult birds to spot. They covet the darkness of the stream, darting along the riverbed amidst the carp and asphalt and china shards. Instead of observing, he has learnt to listen out for the adults' trilling; they never stray too far from the nest.

Christopher cuts a straight line through the swathes of barley, dipped in sun like fine brush heads, careful to only tread down what is necessary. It was his dad who taught him that — to leave the ground as you found it, as though you were never really there. His mum said that was rich for a man who works at a sawmill. His dad will be there now, slicing through the pines' life lines, his palms thick and black as leather. It is unspoken that Chris will work there next summer, when school is finished — that his life will burn long and slow.

He reaches the river and stares at his reflection, swimming disparate and grey among the lily heads and lashing chub until he hears the chicks call out, shrill and desperate and hungry. He turns away from himself.

He wades up to his knees in the dark water with the deft movements of a poacher. If he startles the parents now, he risks the abandonment of the fledglings.

He reaches the bridge and peers into the intricate tapestry of the nest. Yellow mouths gape from the darkness like daffodils emerging from the fetor soil. 'How many? One, two...' Another set of eyes. 'Three.'

Tentatively, he reaches a calloused hand into the nest and removes the first chick, its stunted feathers fanning out, immersing the thin gold band of Chris' wedding ring. It almost escapes between his fingers for a moment, eager to fly too soon, before it acquiesces, playing dead. 'I know, I know.' He places it into his cotton bag and does the same to the other two.

He sets himself on an outcropping of pebbles for a moment, overcome with a sudden exhaustion. He has been prone to these spells recently, where his body becomes limp and very numb, his mind vacuous. He thinks about calling his wife but he left his phone in the kitchen on the way out. She'll still be asleep, anyway; she sleeps in often these days, her spine bent like a lit match. It was her idea to move home, back to the country. She said it would help him find his way back to himself. Still, she gets the worst of him. They argue when there is little to talk about, habitually, like scratching a healing cut; there is too much wood on the hearth, the radio is too loud, he is kicking again in his sleep. When they reconcile, she pats him down like she is putting out a fire in his clothes.

The chicks cry out again, derailing his thoughts. He reaches for his knapsack and pulls out the wire rings and a pair of pliers. His fingers seize momentarily. He was always afraid that he would hurt the chicks when he was a boy. Will they feel it? He would ask his father. How placid the world seemed then, innocuous. He will take his daughter bird ringing when she is old enough to be gentle with them — seven, perhaps eight. She will be dark haired like his mother, he can see it. She will be wilful, and he will love her more for it.

He places the ring around the bird's fragile leg and secures it between the mouth of the pliers. The chick's black eyes flutter shut. *Go on, you won't hurt him Chris...* The snowdrops bow their heads. He should pick fresh flowers for his dad's graveside. There is nobody else to do it now.

He rings the other two chicks, both girls, and places them in his open palms, raising them towards the sky like an offering. He nestles them gently amongst the moss and intertwined grass stems. They cry out again, louder than ever, as he sometimes does in his sleep. They are too young to feel fear, to feel anything other than hunger.

The sky is beginning to darken like a bruise forming beneath the skin. Dawn can't have elapsed to dusk; a storm must be coming. He should tell his mum so she can get the washing in off the line.

He trudges back over to the river's edge and sets himself on the grass, bejewelled with dew. He shivers, his bare feet bitten by the sudden chill. He would've worn his waders if he'd known how cold it was going to get.

A sudden voice crests the hillside, high, shrill, startling him. A woman is walking towards the river, black hair streaming down her back. Her arms are gesticulating wildly; her mouth is wide open. Perhaps she is lost; it is easily done if you come off the path. How lucky he came out today. He'll tell Helen to get her a cup of tea and send her on her way. 'Dad!' Her call coasts low over the valley. 'I found him, Laura, thank god! I found him!'

He'll wait for her to come to him; his limbs are leaden again. He should rest a while. Besides, the dipper mother is back — watching at the periphery, strong against the current. She flits over the water and back to the bank like a stop motion animation, calling out to her young.

The stranger shouts once more, close enough to startle the mother bird. Chris watches her dart over the bank and sink into the field like a seedling. She may be back tonight with food for the hatchlings, he thinks distantly, or she may be on the other side of the valley, seeking a new mate and a different home. It is a simple instinct that compels her.

RECOVERING AFTER BREAKDOWN

Is it possible
We have all become unhealthy   in our greed
For bigger and more
I sit grounded on the floor
Rooted in the old wooden slates of my tiny cottage

There is nowhere here more than three steps from the sofa or the tap
Dripping slightly with clean fresh water like a wound
And the fire heats the whole – singular room
Until my bones start to feel the heat seep
And I feel comforted that I am not feeling my weakness every day
When yesterday I couldn't climb the stairs
Without my body clawing   internal twisted in pain

But here there's only birdsong
And the sofa never more than three steps away

Why did we build bigger

VERSIONS OF MYSELF

My feet are touching the bottom of my bedframe.

They didn't use to, and they don't always. Only when I am sleeping and fully lying down, I can feel my toes touch the wooden frame at the bottom of my bed, even though I am already lying as far up as I can with my hair slightly grazing the top part of the wood. There is no more space for me to go, so my head touches the top and my feet touch the bottom.

When I first got the bed, there seemed to be endless space for my feet to go, and it seemed way too big for me, but my father said I would grow into my big girl bed eventually, and – eventually – I did.

The wall across from me is painted white, with some bubbles on the otherwise smooth surface, because I painted over my wallpaper rather than put a new one on. Even though I felt I had outgrown the elephants, wandering circus, baby blue, I couldn't bring myself to tear it down. So, I painted over it and, under the white paint, the elephants, wandering circus, baby blue are still there.

Now the walls are decorated with pictures and shelves and plants and figurines I collected and white and yellow and green and gold.

There are dents on the floor from my desk chair. A semi-perfect circle a few shades lighter than the hardwood from a nervous habit of turning the plastic wheels of the chair around. It used to stand in front of a small desk that my parents built the summer before I started school while I sat on my too-big bed and watched, because I was too young to help, although I handed them the screws when my dad held out his hand to me. When I was older – I think around the time I turned 15 – I switched out the desk for a vanity and the desk moved into our office, but it was fine because it had become too small for me to the point where my legs barely fit under it. It's now my sister's, whose legs still fit perfectly. The vanity was from IKEA, and I built it myself and I handed myself the screws. I kept the chair and the nervous habit.

A noticeboard, so filled with bits and bobs you cannot make out the cork anymore, but when I need to pin a new piece on there, an empty spot seems to magically appear.

Concert tickets fill up a big part of it, most of them by the same artist. My favourite rapper, seven tickets, my favourite band, three, my favourite singer, one, a live show from my favourite true-crime podcast, one, my favourite singer from when I was twelve, one, a yearly music festival in my hometown, four. One of them from this year, the oldest from 2012, a thin layer of dust over it. One of the bands is no longer together and I haven't listened to the true crime podcast in months. Something about it started to trigger my anxiety, but I miss my Wednesday morning drive to Uni with a newly dropped episode. I now listen to a YouTuber podcast instead.

I've pinned old bracelets on the board that I had to cut off after wearing them for far too long. Some of them frayed out, others are no longer their original colour. No longer needed for access to festivals, or camping grounds, or clubs, but a reminder for myself and others that, yes, I did spend a weekend on this field, miles away from any city and danced in the rain to some not-yet-famous but somewhat well-known indie band, while being squeezed between a stranger on my left and my best friend on my right while holding my pee in for hours because you lose your spot if you go. Driving home exhausted and promising each other to go every year. I have

three bracelets on my board that prove we kept the promise until the tickets became more expensive, and the bands less famous, or we just less familiar with the new music scene, so we decided to treat ourselves to a yearly weekend trip instead, with a hotel room instead of a tent and a spa instead of holding our pee. I have the photos to prove that too.

They are stuck to the back of my door, meticulously arranged to cover every bit of wood. They are a timeline from top to bottom, as I print out a few every year and put them under the already existing ones. You can see my hair grow from the bottom of my jaw to the middle of my back if you move your eyes down, like a flipbook of myself and the evolution of my style. I still have all of the clothes pictured, some of them buried in the back of my wardrobe, never to be touched again until someone decides it is back in style. My family is in some of the pictures, my siblings growing up from top to bottom, starting out significantly shorter than me until my brother towers over me in the last photo he is in. Moments with my friends captured and put on the door, but some of them I do not talk to anymore. But I once did, so they get to stay on there, at least for now.

When you open the door, there is a piece of paper stuck to the frame, drooping down instead of sticking out and barely reaching my chin. When I put it there, it was taller than me and taller than my siblings, which was the important part because you had to be at least this tall to be allowed in my room, myself excluded of course, because it is my room. My sister was fuming, and she put one on her own door, even higher up than mine and we weren't tall enough for the longest time. But now we are, but they would be allowed in my room now, even if they weren't because I was only ten and my siblings were annoying, but they aren't as much anymore, so I don't mind them in my room and I like when they come by and sit with me on my bed.

All the versions of myself that I once was are in this room and the version I am right now will someday also be a version that was. It will remain somewhere in this room, but my feet will never again not touch the bottom of my bedframe.

DIY

to be a *transsexual* is to
reclaim the force
by which you were moulded.
take it into your hands
and grip it tight.
turning it upon yourself,
as yourself
to align your body and
soul.
your body is your own,
craft yourself whole.

ALICE, ADRIFT

It has been five years since we last saw one another, you and I.

That time I was still bright and sharp with hurt, my mask securely in place. London had paralysed me. The sheer force of the crowds, the choking fumes, the catacomb-like claustrophobia of the underground. I had needed to return though, to prove myself in some way. But each corner pub in Soho had ignited an anticipation of trouble in my gut, where I was made the butt of the joke until I combusted. The Seven Sisters bus rekindled the feeling of dread as to what I would find at home.

How could I have been enticed away from you by someone like this?

When we met on that day five years ago, I was lost, deep within my own defences, surrounded with barbs made rusty by alcohol, my old sense of humour withered. You looked at me then, as if you couldn't quite see me.

'So, where next?' you asked, as you shifted in your seat, your attention caught by something through the pub window.

'I've an offer on a cottage. In North Wales. Brutal landscape but beautiful. Peaceful.'

'Sounds ideal.'

'You can see the old quarry from the kitchen. It changes with the light. I might grow stuff.'

'I'll visit once you're settled.'

I shrugged, conditioned by isolation. I could sense you as if from the far side of a chasm. Too far to reach. I was unable to bridge it that day, ashamed of what I had gone through. What I had allowed to happen. My freedom was a desolate prize.

I filled the void with my new home, planting, and tended seedlings until they grew strong. Planted until the space brimmed with colour, texture and scent against the stark, protective slate cliffs.

You did not visit.

In those five years I unlearned the person I had become, but am I the same as I was before?

You are. You occupy the same outline, walk with the same easy grace. You are here, and I am once again filled with that sense of awe for the possibilities. Am I grasping at something of myself within you? Might you have kept a piece of me safe, a piece untainted by the years between?

I remember, so clearly, that first time. Afterwards, you had read to me from your grandmother's copy of *Alice in Wonderland*. I was Alice, adrift in an unfamiliar land of familiar things. You lay there, one arm cradling me, the other holding the book aloft. You had a way of flipping the pages with your left thumb. I could feel the steady rhythm of your heart, and mine calmed in synch with it.

We had been flirting, you and I, for weeks. Glances caught across the table, the current between us when our hands touched as if our nerves fused in conjoint recognition, and the gentle teasing, only possible with deepening knowledge of the other.

One day we drove away from London, to visit your grandmother in the town of wistful spires, whispering courtyards and shoals of bicycles. After tea we sat by the river, expanding the bubble of those last precious moments before the inevitable return. Across the river, a girl lay asleep under a tree, her book collapsed on her belly. Nearby, a rabbit, ears flickering for signs of danger, cropped the grass with neat, mechanical movements.

'Look,' you whispered. 'Alice's adventures are about to begin.'

We orbited one another; two satellites following a mirrored trajectory within our private universe. We walked through midnight and talked through dawn.

Then, the night of the glutinous heat of that London summer. As a crowd, we had drifted across the Heath with the rare, blistering afternoon. We stopped to sit and smoke, spellbound by the hazy view of the city below us, the sounds smudged and distant. Your hand rested on mine for longer than necessary. That moment, the one that comes in the space before two people know for certain. Before even the first kiss stung lips and sent blood charged, racing around the body.

That moment is perfection.

Anything, everything, is possible. The ultimate moment of being, cemented in the here and now, yet infinitely expansive. It is merely a series of hormonal responses: a shot of adrenaline — the same as fear — but mixed with endorphins and it becomes a heady cocktail of bliss. It has the power to dissolve barriers between any two mortals. It transcends gender, race, age. But is this love or lust? It starts the same. But after, love continues acceptance, lust strives to fulfil needs through the other. Or so I have found.

Back at the flat, we sat and smoked in a jumble of cups and biscuit packets, limbs all glowing, sleepy from the sun. Coltrane was our soundtrack as we laughed about the streaker who had run, with pure joy, across the crisp, brown hillside to cheers of admiration. It seemed to define the day. I rose, taking the teapot with me to the kitchen, its fecund body still warm from the last round of tea. The aroma of charred meat drifted in through the open windows from next door's garden, the sounds of laughter and clinking bottles hailing the carnival atmosphere. I didn't hear you follow until you were behind me, whispering my name in my ear. It sent a softness down my neck, through each vertebrae, a message to every nerve. You turned me to face you, held me there, in your gaze as if you were reading my DNA, the map of my soul. Your lips parted as if you might speak, but you stopped, smiled, and then you kissed me.

I had kissed before, and since. Kissed with those whose passion is starving, defiant, possessive. Kissed with determined piracy. Kissed like being branded by a hot iron. You kissed me like someone feeding a beacon on the shore, gradually building the fire to protect the one out at sea. There was nothing selfish in your kiss. You were no wrecker of ships.

We left the kettle to boil — someone else could make the tea — and in silence, slipped into my room. We bathed in the scent of salt and sun-baked skin. We lay in the chaotic landscape of my bed and explored the brief historical maps of our bodies. Here, where your appendix came out, age ten. Here, where I cut my knee falling in my sister's platform shoes, age eight. Here, where your brother tripped you, splitting your right eyebrow, the week your father left; you were fifteen. We did this in whispered reverence, the soft saxophone and laughter from the room next door permeating the wall, but not our space. We traced with lips and fingertips, the contours, curves and recesses, reaching depths uncharted before. And afterwards, *Alice*.

And so we continued in our wonderland for the remainder of that meandering, chimerical summer, until the air shifted and cooled. A party. You, in the arms of another and me, disappearing into the shadows, until only my Cheshire cat smile was left. I told myself I wanted your happiness and hid in the embrace of the next lover. A careless, drunken transposing.

London feels different now. I negotiate buses and tube trains free of the sensation of sinking into a soft grave. London bears a mantle of familiarity, as if viewed through a mirror. Those five years, in which nothing really happened yet everything changed, are distant. Now, after the jangling awkwardness of our last meeting, it is comfortable. We have just left a concert, a casual invitation. No expectations, just two friends, easy in each other's company, grateful for the moments shared.

'I missed you,' you say as we leave. You reach for my hand as if across the years. 'You were so involved. I didn't like to interfere. And then after...'

I stumble into the rabbit hole again, on my way to Wonderland with you once more. My body slackens to the fall.

'I missed you too.' We stall as people flow past us. And you whisper my name in my ear. My senses ebb and what is left is the anticipation of discovery. My name from your lips. There is no twenty years between, just the orbit of our moment.

'I've met someone,' you say, and my heart is pinched and hungry for the feast it can only watch.

'Oh,' I breathe as I wrap my arms around you and squeeze, feeling the *you* within.

'I'm so happy for you. It's what we each hope for, after all.'

Your arms, my safe haven, envelope then release me. Inside, I am Alice, adrift in a sea of my own tears, watching from the raft as the land I will never discover drifts out of reach.

TURNING TIDES

WHAT COMES NEXT

The world has gone almost quiet
in the hours before it will get loud again.
And you'll hear stumbling beneath you on the streets,
the sound of other people's laughter dancing through the air with
         your memories.

But first, you'll sip tea made too weak, by someone you love fiercely.
And you'll walk sugar sticky-fingered down a promenade,
the taste of chocolate on your tongue.

And the sky will melt, molten-lava swirling mess, into a sunset on
         the sea.
And the wind will brush your hair back in time with every other
         breath,
just often enough to remind you that some days you feel alive.

You'll wander until an ache finds solace in your hips,
and turn keys in a door that's not quite home, but home enough.
You'll play music loud and unashamed.
And a phone will carry the tunes of love from a cell line,
a golden string will cross the continents, from your chest to your
         mother's.

The word 'friend' will have new faces.
The word 'hope' will have new horizons too.
And when you picture some idea of a perfect future,
you'll see a blurry splattered disarray that promises to be bright.

Nothing is even sort of certain but
longing and belonging are learning to coexist
somewhere beneath your ribcage.
Being lost and being loved have left their opposing sides.

All of this becoming is so unbecoming,
this mess of being made.
But with each passing week
you are starting to fall in love
with the shape of yourself that you are finding underneath the clay.

And that was more than you could have ever hoped for
not all that long ago.

THE TYRANNY OF TIME

He faces the mirror every day, aware of what awaits him, a player in the world's most tedious game. As promised, he will see it through until the end, no tapping out. Over the years he has learned that the passage of time has its own set of rules and reasons. It has a tight grip and shows mercy to no one – a tyrant betting on everyone's slow demise.

He watches the skin sag, the wrinkles deepen. Occasionally, people tell him that he looks like he had a fulfilled life, pointing out the craterous laugh lines around his eyes and mouth. He nods, laughs along, a cordial old gentleman. Later, he sits down in the living room and contemplates the empty chair in front of their mahogany desk.

His eyes are getting worse. Nowadays, he feels like he is watching the world through a frosted glass window. The milky film bubble-wraps his world into a colourless kaleidoscope. He wishes to go blind, to simply wake up one morning and find that he is absolved of watching the slow decay of his body. New ageing spots appear on his forearms, new varicose veins bulge out of his legs like worms feasting on his corpse.

He sits in the living room a lot. From the familiarity of his armchair, he can observe the weather through the wide window or let his gaze drift over the books on the shelves. Before his eyes started to decline, he used to count them daily – 431 in total. When he gets bored now, he tugs at the oily skin of his hands until it hurts. Recently he noticed that his skin does not snap back anymore. Fleshy mole hills stand out in the vast fields of his fossilised skin. Long seconds pass. His eyes strain as he watches them slowly, ever so slowly, flatten. His body is mocking him, his failing form a testament to a failed life.

He's back in front of the mirror. His wrinkled hands reach out for the stray curl that always finds its way back into his field of vision. He tucks it behind his left ear, only to have it escape its hold again. It used to be black. It's grey now – a sickly shade mirroring the smudges under his equally ashen eyes. Some days, the bags under his eyes are so dark and swollen that he cannot help but laugh. (Insomnia and incontinence will do that to a person.) He sighs, tugs on the skin of his hand, goes back to his armchair, looks at their books with aching eyes.

Today he has a visitor. Today is special. He watches his lover stand behind him through the mirror's reflection, a familiar hand on his shoulder. Their eyes meet in the mirror, clouded grey and dark brown, the colour a near perfect match for the mahogany desk in their living room. The gleam in his love's eyes is youthful, skin unblemished, cheeks rosy. A soft smile spreads across a pretty face. Pearly white teeth peek out behind plump lips. Round and rich, he still remembers how they felt pressed against his own, their honey-sweet taste. These days, only the sourness of the denture glue lingers in his mouth. He begs for more, even as his chest clenches in despair. *Please keep smiling at me like that.*

The following silence hangs thick in the air.

A violent shiver runs through him then. Awareness of his brittle bones returns as his trembling knees knock against each other. His joints hurt after standing for too long. The soles of his feet are sore. Weathered skin feels paper-thin where it touches the frigid air. He thought he had grown to be more enduring over the years, but a mournful sob escapes his lips as he wraps his arms around his frail torso. Trembling fingers clench in the thick wool of his cardigan.

The cold creeps in easily without his beloved's warm eyes watching him.

What a privilege it is to grow old, the empty space behind him whispers.

RUINA

TIKTAALIK OR THE FISH THAT WALKED

O do you remember? when the days were longer
And the sun was hotter
And the ocean bluer?
And blacker too, for O the nights they were darker
And their music louder
Yet the stars were brighter

But on those long days O say, do you remember?
Loping across the sands
Clambering 'round the rocks
In the cracks and crannies you'd creep, remember?
What d'you think you'd find there?
Lunch? O that came later
Watching white waves gnaw the shore, hearing them shatter
The deluged pebbles rasp
In the burning sun bask

Amid blue skies, remember? the sky was wider
And the seas were deeper
And you a keen diver
So dive deep, in reefs where frozen trilobites sleep
Come back for a breather
When the sun sinks lower

PER ASPERA

'I can't see it,' she whimpers, fingers squeezing mine so hard that my parched skin bursts. Sometimes she forgets how strong she is. I place my other hand atop hers and glance over her head.

The horizon is washed into a grey veil by choking clouds of smoke. The inability to see what she will be heading towards terrifies her.

'I know, my little nebula, I know. But it is out there. The stars are out there, too, I promise.' Her green eyes widen, flushing with tears, hands trembling with fear. It breaks my heart to see my child like this.

'We were supposed to see them together.'

I'm caught between telling her a lie, *I'll follow and find you*, or the terrible truth, *I can't come with you*. With every minute wasted on this rooftop, another skyscraper cracks, shatters, and crumbles to the ground in a deafening thunderclap. The Earth keeps throbbing and quivering. I feel the vibrations in my core, in my throat.

After a brief pause, one, two, three, it quakes again with the nauseating feel of *dvumm dvumm...*

I hold my breath and scavenge the distance. No new building cracks.

And then it starts again; one, two, three... *dvumm dvumm...*

This time, a skyscraper falls. The dust clouds are creeping in closer. I finally take a deep breath, and the air of the dying world scorches my lungs.

'You have to let go of me,' I tell her. Snot is streaking down her face, but she is still fighting her tears. My dear, brave child.

'You promised we would see them together.'

'I did. I'm sorry.' I lift my eyes to the once-blue sky, a faint memory I hold from the past. It used to be so beautiful. All I wanted was for my child to see it too. Perhaps not this blue sky that we chased away, but the new one that we built, because that's what we do: we destroy to build, and then we destroy and build some more because we cannot fix our mistakes anymore. I only wish we were faster with this one so I could come with her. I wish I had known today would be the day when it all ends.

My knees buckle and I crouch next to the pod I've tucked her in. The coordinates are ready. I look at her beautiful face, desperately trying to catalogue her every molecule to think of when I go, but then my eyes meet hers and I don't want to remember her like this. Her expression mirrors the burning accusation I harboured towards my mom and dad. They lounged in front of the television every single evening to learn what tragedies happened during the day, to follow the countdown of our days. As a child, the images on the screen saddened and terrified me to no end. The newscasters talked a lot about the future. My parents said they were fearmongers and I shouldn't worry, but I worried nonetheless.

Now, my daughter's eyes reflect the rage I felt at them for delivering me into a world like that.

A sharp pain lashes through my chest, but then I recall the day we went to the visionarium together and she learnt about green grass and the stars. Oh, the stars... I'd never seen her that excited before. The exhibition showed the world that they had been creating out there for us — a world that was mirrored after ours from before it started falling apart.

'Mom, are those... Are those real?' She asked me, eyes wide and mouth agape as pictures of the stars speckled all around us.

'They are,' I said, squeezing her hand.

'They sparkle.'

I smiled. 'They do. When we move to our new home, we'll be able to see them every single night.'

She tore her gaze away from the holograms and gave me an astonished look. 'Really?'

'Yes, I promise.' Her eyes shone with galaxies of joy and, for the first time, the guilt that had been clutching me started to ease.

I choose to remember her in those moments, and in the ones I will never live to see, the ones that only existed in the hopes of my dreams: of her, amongst the stars, in a new world of old miracles. Even as I hold her aching gaze, I find solace in knowing that she'll have the future I promised her — I just won't be there with her.

One, two, three... *dvumm dvumm...*

'My little nebula,' I say as I touch a button on the control panel that closes the pod's shield almost as quickly as it takes me to stand up. 'You have to go now.'

Her iron-will snaps at last, and she screams, hammering her fists against the window. She abuses the same button on the panel but all of it is in vain because there is no turning back for her. 'Mom!' She yells in one last desperate breath.

I take in those beautiful green eyes once more.

One, two, three... *dvumm dvumm...*

My heart shatters into a million tiny pieces.

Even if I had the time, I wouldn't know how to pour into words all that I feel for her, so I just mouth *I love you*, and witness as the engine starts up and then —

One, two, three... *dvumm dvumm...*

I feel the vibration of the waning world right beneath my feet.

Her pod lifts off and just like that, she shoots towards a horizon covered in dust.

One, two, three... *dvumm dvumm...* The concrete cracks between my shoes.

'See the stars, my little one, see the stars for the both of us.'

SEE YOU IN SPACE, COWBOY

UP IN THE HEAVENS

Saturday night starts as theirs often do, quiet and polite, straight-backed at dinner, their burning hands snatched out from each other's as soon as grace is said. Sadie makes sure to always say please and thank you to Mrs Pierce, and when Clarissa's father asks if she'll let Cooper from next door take her out again, she laughs like her heart isn't pounding and her palms aren't sweating. Then it's time to do the dishes, soapy hands and stolen glances. Her parents wish them goodnight, making them promise not to stay up late so that they're fresh for Church come the morning, and Clarissa smiles, the muscle in her jaw so tense it might snap.

It's only later, when the light seeping in from under the doorway goes dark, and her mother's footsteps recede upstairs, punctuated with the click of a closing door, that Clarissa feels like she can breathe. She falls back onto her bed with a sigh. Sadie, sitting on the edge of her chair, stops pretending to be interested in the pages strewn haphazardly across Clarissa's desk. Their eyes meet and the space between them crackles.

Clarissa whispers for her to come closer. Her voice is unstable, punctuated with tiny puffs of air that come fast and shallow. Then Sadie is moving, curling over her like she can block out the whole world's eyes.

The scent of apple shampoo overwhelms her, and she scarcely has time to draw a breath before a warm mouth closes over hers and any thoughts of breathing are banished from her mind. She runs her hands through Sadie's long, dark hair, scratching her nails gently at her scalp and delighting at the shudder it pulls from her.

'Clara,' Sadie mumbles against her lips, her fingers twisting the thin cotton of Clarissa's shirt.

She pulls away but stays close, eyelids heavy as she drinks in the sight of her. Her cheeks, sprinkled with freckles, blush rose petal pink as she watches Clarissa watching her.

It is there, looking up at Sadie, faces framed by the curtain of Sadie's hair, their skin flushed, and their legs intertwined, that something inside Clarissa shifts. Sadie gazes down at her, her eyes bright and her mouth parted. Her eyelashes flutter against the tips of her cheeks with every blink, and she is even more beautiful in the soft lamplight; the flickering warm glow illuminating the contours of her face.

Clarissa feels the change within her; something nestled in deep, stretching and unfurling. The feeling spills out through her chest, warm and heavy like spiced wine, filling her veins, rich and intoxicating and important.

'I'm in love with you,' she hears herself say, and it doesn't scare her like she thought it would. Sadie's eyes snap to hers and Clarissa is granted the unique wonder of watching the realisation spread across her face.

'What?' Sadie breathes, her eyes almost comically wide.

She nods, pulling her lip between her teeth to stop herself from grinning.

'You're –' Sadie cups her face between her palms, sinking her knees into the plush mattress on either side of Clarissa's hips. 'With me?'

'Yes.'

'Really?'

Clarissa laughs. 'Yes, of course, *really*.'

Sadie laughs too, breathless and bubbling out of her as she

kisses her forehead, each one of her cheeks, the cold tip of her nose. 'I love you too,' she breathes, 'Of course, I love you, Clara.'

Everything else slips away, nothing left but two souls pressed against each other. Clarissa can see the tiny shadow of doubt in Sadie's face, like she doesn't quite know if she believes her, but she desperately wants her to. That's alright. Clarissa has a lifetime to prove it to her. For the first time in her life, Clarissa finds herself unable to care what anyone might say; not her mother, or her father, and not even God. Let them drone of fire and of brimstone. She has heaven in the palm of her hand.

WOMAN

supplicated on the kitchen floor
the curling wand is today's chisel.
I have given up on the brushes
except to black out the gaps in my eyebrows.

silver, not gold.
and I never wear red unless it's rope
and then it's *cherry, cherry, cherry.*
I know how to use my hands.

soft in scent of english roses,
I give cocoa butter kisses to the dog
right between his dumb little bug eyes
and know I love him more than I'll ever love a man.

teenage me would have sneered
at my nail tech, a father's simile,
but now I love her 'cause she's kind,
waxes poetic about my nail beds.

ink of iris bitten into a thigh
so even my pain is botanical
blushed up pretty, *liquid plum*,
I am the sin worth tasting.

CONSTRUCTIVE NOTES FROM OVERLY-ATTACHED NIGHTMARES

There are things in the dark.

This is the first thing you learn as a child. You learn it independently, without anyone having to tell you, from the evidence of your own eyes and ears. There are things in the dark; they move just beyond your range of sight, but perhaps, one day, they won't.

You spend the rest of your life trying to unlearn this.

You are small and weak and ill-suited to the world, as the world constantly reminds you, so your childish understanding of shape and form could be a symptom of your own imperfect self. It is entirely possible that the entire human race somehow developed the same bug in their genetic code. But I would advise against relying on this theory too much. I would advise against closing your eyes to the shadows, or turning away, or pretending you don't see anything.

We don't like to be ignored.

We remember when you were young, younger than you are now, and you came home so late that your mum sent you to bed without tea. You huddled, sniffling as though no one could hear you, buried beneath a mountain of blankets. You didn't want to play that night. That wasn't very nice of you. You had already added to your mother's collection of grey hairs and now there you were, wallowing away in self-pity instead of scanning the darkness for our skittering, scratching movements.

(It's Sheila who does the skittering, by the way. She's very proud of it. If you even care.)

Jimmy had the lightning bolt of inspiration that night. He waited until you were properly tuckered, your tears winding down. Probably you had a headache, even as you started to drift off, so it's likely you felt it like a screw tightening in your skull when that stack of books on your desk – you know, the ones you bumped close to the edge when you came storming through the door in a mard? – came tumbling down. The crash was not quiet.

We all saw you freeze. We saw the tiny fingers reach up to the covers, debating whether to pull them back and take a peek. That's when Jane decided to breathe, very deeply, just above where your head would emerge. It could have been a draft, but it wasn't.

(It was Jane. We all were impressed with that one. Well done, Jane.)

The best part about that night was that you were in trouble, so you couldn't even go to your mum for help. You were stuck there until the sun spilled under the curtains, with us.

(We were working very hard that night. You ignored us. Your fault.)

We have to say that some of our favourite memories were when you stopped spending all your nights in your room.

(It took longer than most people; we weren't sure if you noticed.)

The stars in the city aren't as bright as they are at home. We would watch you, standing on a street corner with your head tilted back, trying to pick out the constellations you know. There aren't very many: The big dipper, the little dipper and, sometimes, Orion's belt. It's unclear to us if you ever spotted any or if they were lost in the glow of the streetlights. We didn't help much; big heavy footsteps on the pavement are one of our specialties.

Even when your friends arrived, twenty minutes late and buzzed from something you weren't invited to, we followed you out into the night. We watched you realise that your friends had given up on us, stopped believing in things in the dark. How lonely must their little lives be without us hiding just out of sight?

They aren't safe from us. You know that. You watched us for them, all those nights, guarding them from the dark and the things that live in it. Bad things will happen if you look away.

('Bad things' is Helen's department, and she is very efficient. Remember when your mum fractured her spine the day you didn't check your feet on the pavement? Helen got a certificate.)

We did take one holiday. It was when you moved out into that rat-infested flat, sleeping on that floor mattress. You put on such a brave face when your partner told you about the rats, we were very proud of you. All rolled-up sleeves, pushing the mattress up against the wall and volunteering to sleep on the outside. We want to let you know that we saw you – the tension in your body every night, the jump whenever your partner brushed against you, the hitch in your breathing if you heard a skitter.

(Sheila felt a little professionally threatened by the rats. She considered retirement for a week or two, but in the end she decided she just loved the job too much.)

You had learnt to do our work for us. It's very rare that we all decide to take a holiday together, but we had so much faith in you that we went ahead and booked a two-week stay at *Disneyland*, which we spent reminding parents how much everything cost and how much their children would resent them if they didn't buy it. It was incredibly refreshing, but we did miss you.

All this is to say that we do value you. The many years of our professional relationship have meant a lot to us, and we hope you share our enthusiasm for its continued growth.

(You need us. Where the hell would you be without us?)

So, you can understand that when we came back from *Disneyland* to find the rats gone, the mattress elevated, and you putting on those fancy new work clothes, we felt a little betrayed.

That's not to say we gave up. We didn't. We all put in the hours. Sheila skittered her heart out. Jimmy pushed over more precariously-balanced objects than we knew you had. The straw that broke the camel's back for them was finding out you had bought a cat. There was no real coming back after that.

(Their last day was tearful. We all pitched in to buy them a bottle of rosé for all their hard work. You didn't even notice when Jimmy dropped it on the floor, just shook your head at General Scratches and smiled as you cleared it up.)

Brad was our star in that time. He spent so many hours sat on your bedroom floor, reminding you of all the times you stuttered talking to a stranger, every time a joke fell flat, every time you talked too long or too fast or too quiet. Together with Helen, they formed a dream team. They brainstormed all the creative ways you could mess up your budding relationship, reminded you of the too-few things that would have to go wrong for the rent to be unpaid, suggested articles about people your age in six-figure jobs with a house and no mortgage and all the many, many ways you were unlike them.

(We do love you, that's why we try to be realistic with you. Who are you trying to impress?)

It is rude to ignore your colleagues. We try not to take things like this personally, but it's difficult when we've all had such a close working bond over the years. Your future matters to us and, clearly, your vision of the future is a home you don't fear, supported by a job that doesn't demoralise you, sustained by strong and stable emotional connections, instead of you, in a small dark room, hiding from shadows. Many people would call these differences irreconcilable, but we remain hopeful that you will see the error of your ways.

(You made Helen cry, you git.)

We write to you now, collectively, not to shame you but to urge you to think. The next time you go to bed, lean into that shiver running down your spine. Jane worked hard on that. Squint your eyes and see if you can make shapes out of furniture. Wonder if that noise was really the cat. Think about what would happen to your darling partner if you drifted off and all was not as it seems. It pays for our work to be appreciated.

(Please don't ignore us. We only want your attention.)

Kind regards,

Your Overly-Attached Nightmares

WINGS OF A BUTTERFLY

Thick, ugly thoughts. Don't be too loud. Whatever you do, don't stop smiling. We want you to be independent and stable, but not *too* independent that you no longer need us. That's not how this works. You must pay your taxes but be careful, don't work too much, otherwise you'll be a bad mother, a terrible partner, a greedy workaholic. Please cook, clean, make yourself pretty for us. Wear the skirt that makes your legs look amazing – don't reveal too much, otherwise, you'll be a tart. Remember, don't stop smiling.

You wonder if the trees demand the same of the grass. 'Look greener, stop wilting.' Does the sky get annoyed at the clouds for eclipsing its magnificent blue?

'Are the clouds not insufferable?' the sky says. 'Look at them, so fat and grey.'

Perhaps the bees defend themselves ('they were asking for it') because the flowers are so luscious – their petals soft and inviting – the bees couldn't help themselves. In the woods, a bear scratches itself against a tree and doesn't ask for permission. The sharp bark feels amazing against its coarse winter coat, shedding for the summer months. As the bear continues rubbing against the trunk, it dreams about salmon – it does not worry about next winter. Why should it? There is no point in worrying about the inevitable.

Your bank balance stares at you from your phone screen under the table.

'Would you like the salmon?' a male voice jerks you out of your thoughts and you look up. The man sitting opposite you is wearing a white shirt and a red tie. It reminds you of blood from a fresh wound. You would love the salmon, but it is too expensive. The bear doesn't have to worry about the price of the fish. You wonder if the man is planning on paying the bill (you hope so).

'I'll have the mackerel,' you say to the waitress hovering next to the table. Her lipstick is too pink for her complexion, and her nail polish is chipped.

When was the last time you were truly happy? Perhaps that trip to Corfu, with your ex, before he lost his job and it all changed. Does the sand feel abused when the sea thrashes against it? Pulling and dragging against the grains, changing the very shape of it until it's unrecognisable.

'Perhaps a white wine? It would pair well with fish,' the man says. You hate white wine. Too vinegary and sharp.

'That would be lovely.'

Don't forget to smile.

You smile at the man, and then up at the waitress, who's still hovering, as if she can't wait to leave. You don't blame her. This whole experience is tedious.

Food and drinks ordered, she finally departs. You wish you could leave with her. You can't even remember what the man ordered (stupid girl, you need to pay attention to that sort of thing).

The beach in Corfu had been endless miles of glistening coastline. Even the ocean there acted as if it were on holiday. Lazy waves that crept up the shore, tickling and gentle. Not like the sea back home. The men were charming, and the women were happy. Not like back home.

'So, what do you do for a living?'

Ah, the classic line of questioning – he'll ask what university you studied at next.

'I'm a freelance editor,' you say. Don't forget to ask him questions (they love talking about themselves). 'W-what do you do?'

'Oh, interesting. I'm in finance, have been for seven years now – I just love numbers,' the man's monotonal voice is hard to concentrate on; the words a low hum that seeps into your ears and trickles straight back out. 'If you have the right formula, you can predict next year's net profit, even overheads...'

Your thighs are chafing from where they're squished inside your pencil skirt – a size too small, but you have to fit in it to still be the 'right' size. If the scale increases by one number, you may as well accept your spinsterhood. You wonder if flowers worry about their petal size. Does fruit feel self-conscious as it ripens? Thickening and growing, so plump and fertile, desperate for their seeds to be consumed and dispersed. Do they feel shame? We don't want you plump; you must be thin, but not too thin, in case you cause people to worry. You have to be curvaceous, but only in the right places.

Your drinks arrive; an enormous glass, teetering on a thin pedestal, with a splash of white wine in the bottom and a stout tumbler filled with whiskey. It's a different waitress, a larger lady who smells strongly perfumed and is heavy-handed with your drink. You wonder if the other waitress asked to swap tables – as if your misery's contagious. The man raises his glass to yours, clinking them together.

'Where did you study?'

There it is. He wants you to have gone to university, a prestigious one, but not better than where he went. Did he say where he studied? You should have been paying closer attention.

'Durham.'

His eyes narrow. Wrong answer.

Distract him, smile extra wide, squeeze your arms together to flash your cleavage, but not too much.

'Lovely, um, yes, good for you,' his eyes remain locked on the slither of skin you subtly revealed between your breasts. Perfect. You're like a caterpillar; cocooned and concealed, only to suddenly reemerge with tantalising patterns and glorious wings.

Your fish arrives. Its head is intact – its dead eye gazing up at you from where it lies across the plate, frozen in perpetual horror. The man's own eyes have finally dragged away from your chest to his meal; a fillet of steak, surrounded by glistening potatoes and asparagus. Blood oozes from it, trickling to surround the vegetables. You can see a hole in the mackerel's jaw, where a hook penetrated when it was caught. What an inhumane way to die. Dragged from your home by a piece of metal through your face. The way it must have flapped and squirmed, desperate to return to the watery depths. Did it suffocate? There are no other marks on its scaled body, except a deep gash where its guts were pulled out.

'I studied in Warwick, great place for econ,' he says, stabbing his steak and pulling the flesh apart. Fresh blood spills out. The colour matches his tie. His mouth opens and the chunk of meat disappears, his jaw working so he can speak again. 'I moved back to be closer to my family. At our age, we really must be there for our parents.'

So many presumptions he's already made about you, just from a photo on an app, your age written in discreet font beneath it. But you agree with him because having similar values is more important than your opinions.

Do bears converse while they gobble down salmon? Plants photosynthesise silently, considerate of the other plants around them. You wish you were a butterfly, with a delicate tongue for tasting sweet nectar. The mackerel's eye won't stop staring at you. If you were a butterfly, you could fly far, far away. No more apps, no more overpriced restaurants, you wouldn't have to sit across from a man who doesn't care about you – a man who just wants an accessory, someone to warm his bed and spread her legs, to say all the right things and keep his ego inflated.

'Don't forget to smile,' your mother's voice echoes in your head. 'You'll be alone forever with that sour face.'

You don't want to smile anymore. You don't want to make yourself smaller so that you're easier to swallow. You're tired of apologising to make other people feel more comfortable. You've had enough of gauging what they want from you so that you can keep them happy. This never-ending game of being the perfect 'thing'. Because you are a disposable object who will never live up to such impossible expectations. You are a fish, caught, beaten, and abused, who looks at your captor and says, 'I'm sorry. I seem to have dirtied your hook.'

As a child, when a boy smacked or mocked you, it was because he liked you. Your own mother was convinced the boy next door fancied you because he used to try and spit on you. A few years ago, he was arrested for beating his wife. Her jaw was fractured, and her left eye lost its vision. Her beautiful petals torn; her wings clipped. Is that love? If so, you don't want it.

'What did you just say?'

Shit.

'Excuse me, I need to go to the restroom.'

'Go ahead,' he says. 'Powder your nose and all that!'

You don't smile.

Gathering your small bag, you walk away, making it around a corner until he's out of view. You pass the sign to the bathroom; you don't stop until you're outside. Don't look back. Just keep walking.

You keep walking until eventually, you grow wings, and you fly far, far away.

REJOICE

SPROUTS

They say that the best time to plant flowers is in autumn. Plant bulbs in autumn and, by the spring, you'll have a garden rich with colour. This always seemed a little bit counter-productive to me. Why plant something just before winter – wouldn't the germinating bulbs struggle to survive in the hard, cold soil? Wouldn't the frost kill them dead before they had a chance to creep up and out of the earth?

Still. That's what they say, so that's what I do. I kneel over the flower bed in October with my coat on and hat pulled down firmly over my ears, and I plant my bulbs in neat little rows. I diligently cover the beds with mulch before the frost hits. Winter comes and snow covers the ground, and I think about the things I have planted, struggling to survive. I stand out in the cold and scrape snow off the beds and look for any signs of life, but there's nothing to see. All through December and January, I worry about my little plants deep down in the ground, with no way of knowing if they've begun to sprout roots.

In late February, things finally begin to get interesting. A hint of colour tiptoes up out of the dirt, barely a fingertip's width. But it's something, the first sign I've had. Soon enough, more of the bulbs begin to sprout, until I have about ten signs of life. This, I know, is a crucial time. I cross my fingers that the worst of the cold is over, and God must look kindly on me because no more frosts come, and my plants begin to grow.

The little sprouts grow all through March, climbing upwards day by day. They make slow progress, but the sunlight helps. The warmer it gets, the faster they seem to grow, until one day I wake up and they're all over two centimetres tall, standing up proudly. Around them, weeds grow much faster, their green bodies hurling themselves skywards and threatening to choke out my tiny little fighters. I invest in a good pair of gardening gloves and pull out anything that could threaten my plants. The weeds' green shoots are easy to spot next to the brown of the soil and the soft pink of my plants, but they're hard to keep on top of.

It's April when I venture outside to find that one of my precious stems is leaning dangerously. I try coaxing it back upright, offering it a bamboo stick, stuck into the ground to lean on, but it's no use. The very next day the plant is curled up on itself, a few days after that it collapses completely and is swallowed up by the soil.

Its nine siblings seem to grow faster than ever, and I record their progress eagerly. The April showers do them good. I fuss about drainage and worry about the wind blowing them over, but they seem to flourish in the moist air.

By May, I realise that these plants were never going to flower in spring, but I've already forgiven them for it. They seem to be doing just fine – their spindly little limbs are getting thicker and stronger, and I stop worrying as much about the weeds once they finally begin to outgrow them. They're all almost ten centimetres tall now, soft peachy pink and fleshy, ending with a rounded-off bud where the flower will bloom.

Another one succumbs to the weeds when I least expect it, and I dig the whole bulb out of the ground. It's the first time I can see the part of the growing process that's taking place underground, and I feel a strong rush of affection for my plants, and a stronger desire than ever to see them flower.

In June, one flowers prematurely. The closed palm of the bud opens overnight, and when I first see it, I'm delighted. I'm still in my dressing gown, but I rush back indoors to get changed and to grab my trowel, planning on carefully pulling it from the earth. I don't realise something's wrong until I get back and actually examine the flower. I notice how tiny its little fingers are, how crooked they look. I decide to leave it, hoping it'll get stronger if it's left longer, but soon it shrivels and dies.

I'm on tenterhooks in July. Finally, the remaining seven plants are fully grown, and I can see their buds swelling, ready to burst open. When I'm not watching the flower beds I make all the necessary preparations, buy all the supplies. When that first plump palm opens, when I first see those five perfect little fingers tipped with perfect little fingernails grasping up to the sky, I begin to cry.

I don't even bother with the trowel, and grasp it by the hand. The fingers curl around mine. The soil is just loose enough that I can pull it free. Up, up, and up she comes. First the shoulder, then the head, then the rest of her dirt-covered body. I scoop her into my arms, cradling her. Her tiny eyes blink open, her first look at the sun after nine months in the earth, and she begins to wail.

I feed her and wrap her in blankets and lay her down to rest. And then I wait, eagerly, for her six siblings to bloom.

BUTTERFLY

Rippled out, they
carry my tune,
like crickets in grass
or an old country
rhyme.
But I don't feel like
me, I feel like
a stranger.
Like someone I knew
but couldn't remember.

A butterfly, fresh,
cocooned and refreshed.
I should spread my wings
and find somewhere new.
Find some home comfy
and fluffy, find a new
crew.

But it won't be easy,
like the butterfly told
me, I'm only a
stranger, a useless
fool.

Perhaps just like a
butterfly I'll become

anew, spread my wings
far and wide and
find my own crew.
For now I will lay in
comfort and warmth
and plan my journey
like I thought
I should.

CURSED SEAS

First Day

I woke gasping, wet, thrashing. I opened my mouth and sucked in salty water. Something hard brushed against my hand. It was metal. I grasped it and hauled myself forward. Sunlight stung my eyes as I burst from the water's surface.

I don't remember climbing onto the buoy. No, I remember looping my arms through the frame and vomiting salt-water into the ocean. Bile burnt my lips. There was a hollow pain in my chest, my lungs felt strained as if they'd been stretched out and pulled taut. The muscles in my neck moved despite myself as I retched into the water. Pain, exhaustion and panic merged into a wall of pure sensation. Another retch rocked me. Bile and seawater came up from my gut and filled my mouth. With all the strength I had, I forced my mouth closed and gulped down the putrid liquid, if only so I could have control over myself.

My body continued to shudder as my stomach rejected its contents. Bleary-eyed, I looked around. I could not see the driftwood I'd clung to through the night. All I could see was blue, sea, and sky. No clouds blotted the air. There was no sign of the storm that had sunk my ship.

Suddenly, I found myself sitting, dry-eyed, in the hollow beneath the frame.

Second Day

I slept in the shade of the metal frame. I drifted off before sunset and woke long after sunrise, noon through noon. I did not see the moon or feel the cool night air. Once I had composed myself, I stripped my clothes, still soaked from my night adrift, and hung them from the metalwork to dry.

Thirst pulled at my tongue which clung to my dry mouth.

With nothing else to occupy my time I swam, but never ventured far from the buoy. I saw nothing in the deep. No fish or whale, shark or seabird passing overhead. I was alone, totally alone. Thirst knotted my gut and twisted my throat. I thought of swallowing. Returning to the buoy, I slept.

Third Day

Again, I slept before sunset and woke at noon. No signs of life yet.

I stayed on the buoy, trying not to think about thirst, the song of waves behind me. Ocean called to me. The cool on my skin, the wetness in my throat. Thinking, *don't look at it.*

There is paint peeling from the metal frame. I stripped the patches into patterns.

Mustn't look back.

Fourth Day

I held my tongue out in the water, ripples splashing on my face, just to enjoy the wetness even if it stings my gums. *I mustn't swallow,* I think to myself. The water is poison; cool, beautiful poison. My stomach twisted as the waves cupped my jaw.

I ground my face against the frame. Focus on the pain, put the hunger away for now. Put the thirst away.

Fifth Day

The day was spent in the sea. Stinging my eyes. Surfacing only to breathe. I flee from the sun's tyranny into the cold beneath the waves.

Sixth Day

I have taken a small joy in scratching the dried, sunburnt skin that peeled off my forearms. Flakes, bone white, came away, falling like snow. For the spots I couldn't reach, I dragged myself over the metal framework. Like a snake, shedding, wriggling on rocks. I coiled around the bars, rubbed the small of my back. Beneath, the virgin skin was pink, smooth, hairless. It felt like warm plastic.

There's a jagged piece of metal, jutting from the frame. Blood wells where it scratched me. I lapped it up hungrily. Wetness, joyous. When the blood was gone, I went to the spike. Reaching up, I put my arm to it and pushed hard.

I stopped myself.

Looking over the sea, I wondered. I weighed the options in my head. Wait for salvation that never comes, swim into the dark below. Surround myself with it, cover myself with it.

Water water everywhere, I think to myself.

Seventh Day

There aren't sharks in these waters. There's nothing at all. Nothing to fear in the water. I wonder why I avoided it for days.

I let myself float in the water, head beneath the surface. My eyes open, burning. The cut on my arm screams as the salt fills it. There's blue all around, nothing else. Floating, weightless, there is no up or down, forward or back, there is only blue and me. I dive deep and look sky-ward. Sunlight streams through the waves, a checkerboard of blinding white.

As my lungs strain, I think of opening my mouth. Gulping down the cool water. Feeling the cold pool through me. To drink, to fill my belly that squeezed around nothing.

I open my mouth and hold the cursed water there. I let it fill every part it can reach. It soothes my parched, cracked lips and burns my gums as it fills the invisible gaps between my teeth.

When I return to the buoy, I am refreshed. I don't recall if I swallowed. But lying there, teeth stinging, staring at the sun, I'm not quite so thirsty anymore.

Eighth Day

Ninth Day

I struggle to tell you what's happening, because nothing is happening. No change, no difference, neither improvement nor deterioration. The sun does not set. It doesn't rise either. It's always noon.

It's unbearable, the terrible monotony of dying. Each moment is indistinguishable from the last. I sit and I stew on the buoy, I wait for clouds that do not come. I fall asleep at high-noon, I wake at high-noon. Sometimes I slip into the sea and cool myself for a while. Then I return and sit and wait. If anything changed, it would be terribly exciting. I pray for a gull, or an albatross, or a duck. Not to eat, though that would be tremendous, no, just to look at. The thought of fowl makes my stomach squeeze taut.

Tenth Day

Atop the buoy, the iron, bent outward, intrigues me. The metal is brown with rust, bubbling red paint peeling away. Frequently, I consider pressing my palm onto the shaft, dragging my wrist across the edge. Blood dripping down my skin. Invisible on the paint. Dripping myself into the sea. Lure a shark to me. Float in the water, thrash like a seal, close my eyes and wait.

I couldn't hunt it. Do I want it to kill me? I don't think I do. Maybe I'm just bored again.

Eleventh Day

There was a pile of my dead-skin on the edge of the buoy, waves lapping at it. I crawled over to it on all fours. I dragged my tongue over the pile, lapping up the dried shedding. It tasted of salt and paint. After that, I smiled all day.

Twelfth Day

I don't sleep in the shade, no, I sleep under the sun. Each time I wake, more of my red skin is peeling away and I delight to strip it from me. Once I took a leaf from elbow to wrist, in one long pull. It was a glorious ecstasy, to take it in one smooth motion.

I held the peel in front of my face and stared at the sun through the translucent sheet. The air seemed to shake, but then I realised I was laughing. Laughing at the strip of me, billowing in the air. I opened my mouth and swallowed it, smiling.

Thirteenth Day

My thoughts keep wandering.

Fourteenth Day

I dragged the back of my forearm over the iron spike. Skin drew up as I brought my arm down. Teeth clenched tight at the pain. The sensation was sharp and sore, then cold, then wet as blood dribbled down the raw flesh.

Then I sat, bleeding onto the metal, tasting the blood on my fingertips. A moment of lucidity surfaced, and I questioned myself. Why had I done it? Because I could? Because it was my decision to make? But as quickly as it came, the moment passed, and I returned to licking my arm.

Fifteenth Day

Are the days passing? I haven't seen the night sky. Or dawn or dusk. The sun stays in the same place. It does not move. I stare at it. I stare at the sun until all the colour drains from the world and my eyes sting. And I keep staring.

Sixteenth Day

I sob without tears. The hairs on my neck have grown into an awful beard. When I catch my reflection in the sea, I don't know the strange person looking back at me. I'd give anything for a razor to chop this awful thing off. The sun becomes a haze of orange, then purple, then green, then I wake the next day, with a circular spot hanging in my vision.

I want to cry, scream, hold my head beneath the waves. I'm just so tired.

Seventeenth Day

Land could be just over the horizon. I could swim that far, if I pushed myself. But even the thought of that effort exhausted me. I knew I ought to try, but I just couldn't. The synapses fire, signals scream for me to move, to try, but terminate before becoming action. I lay there, screaming at myself, laying there, despite it all.

Eighteenth Day

I slept today.

Nineteenth Day

MOON CHILD

Perhaps at one time in his life, Amadeo Zylerburg would have told many stories.

But now there is only one.

The children who make up his audience stare at the great wrinkles of his face, at the layers of life wrapped around his eyes. The nearby firelight makes them sparkle with stolen, stubborn youth.

Perhaps that is why the children wait patiently for him to speak.

Perhaps that is why Amadeo tells his story.

It was said that Ayhana was a child of the moon.

It was said that her skin glowed with starlight stolen from the smooth darkness of her hair. It was said that she moved through the trees as swiftly as a stream flows through the soil and as gracefully as a sapling in the wind. It was said that her voice could coax caterpillars from their cocoons and wolves from their dens.

This is simply not true, children.

Ayhana was merely a clumsy human. Ayhana's skin could be rather dull, even in moonlight, and, dear children . . . she really could not sing. We always glorify the dead with their better selves, but I will not do you that disservice.

Ayhana was a child of the moon in name only. In all else, she was sunlight, stolen moments, and dirty bare feet. Her spirit was much like a spirit drink—too strong to swallow but too precious to spit out. Above all, she was fleeting, difficult to grasp, like someone who was always looking for a way out.

She lived in the forest, and it was there that she managed to grow into a strong young woman. Strong enough to catch the attention of a foolish boy from the other side of the village. He saw her wander through the forest one day, and upon taking in all that sunlight, stolen moments, and bare feet, he knew her to be the one.

Ayhana saw him as another foolish village boy, of course. It was for this that she decided to test his foolishness and perhaps his devotion.

One full moon, she led him to a pond at the heart of the forest. In the darkness, the pond looked like a fallen star, or perhaps a delicious bowl of milk. It was said that the pond was cursed, haunted by the ghosts of old forest spirits. Ayhana had never really believed such nonsense, knowing only how cool the pondside moss felt beneath her bare feet. Stubborn girl.

'Swim in this pond with me,' she said as she waded in. 'If you don't, I'll know you aren't the one for me.'

Well, what else could the boy do? He jumped in without a second thought, the cool water washing over his skin, and felt the burning ember of Ayhan's attention as he resurfaced. She looked him up and down and said he was stupid. But also brave.

Within the year they were married.

Ayhana was not a gentle woman, dear children. She burned with rage sometimes, she fought the foolish village boy as fiercely as she fought herself. But she loved deeply. She let him know her. She savoured his name like a prayer she might never say again. She told the boy, once, that worms had taste buds. She would give them all her best table scraps and watch them crawl over the apple peels. She wondered if a spider mourned the loss of its web. Children, I need not tell you how cobwebby their cottage became after that. It drove the village boy to distraction.

She would never sing to the village boy, but she decorated his time with her whistles and hums. She was not a touchy person, but when he embraced her, she was the last to let go. She never said 'I love you' to that village boy, but she would always say that she was as a part of him as grass is a part of the soil, as a tree is a part of a forest. You can't see the wind after all, but you can see the rustling of the leaves, feel it on your face. Her existence made him breathe easier, anger slower, love harder. She loved quietly and *grandly,* dear children, so much that the air came alive with it.

As months became years, Ayhana started to weaken. Her sunlight no longer shone as brightly, her stolen moments felt too fleeting, and even her dirty bare feet had trouble carrying her where she wanted to go. The village boy took her to a nearby medicine woman for help.

'That water is indeed cursed,' the woman said as she put a hand on Ayhana's damp forehead. 'She must have swallowed some. The old forest spirits are bitter and like to torment humans with a long, slow death.'

'What can be done?' the village boy asked desperately.

'To be healthy, she must become a forest spirit herself,' the medicine woman said.

The village boy was about to protest, but then Ayhana put a gentle hand on his arm. 'I am going soon, darling,' she sighed. Her eyes already seemed to hold a new horizon in them, a place only she could see. 'Perhaps we should listen. Perhaps this is what must happen.'

The village boy finally nodded, knowing he could not stop her even if he'd wanted to. He thought back to how she'd fed the worms; perhaps now she was remembering her place on their menu. Besides, she burned too bright for the nonsense of a slow, painful death anyway.

'She shall spend the rest of her life as a forest spirit—a wolf.

Only when the full moon turns the pond as pale and shiny as an opal can she return to human form,' the medicine woman said, already mixing the spell between her fingers.

'Hold me,' Ayhana murmured to the village boy. He did, even when she resisted his touch, even when her eyes forgot his face, even when her fingers clawed and tore at his shirt, even when her voice was no longer her own. She always did like to make a great fuss, dear children, and this transformation was no exception.

Upon the next full moon, when Ayhana shed her wolf skin, the village boy held her again. They met on a hill overlooking the forest, where they could track the moon across the sky. She would speak about her adventures with the forest spirits. She told him how bitter they'd been when humans began encroaching in their territory. She said their anger had been passed down through the generations like a hand-me-down shirt. 'It's too big for them,' she explained one evening. 'And terribly out of fashion. Much like the one you're wearing now . . .'

Children, even as a forest spirit, Ayhana was not a gentle woman. But the village boy did change his shirt and was all the better for it.

In the days without Ayhana, the village boy searched for another cure, another medicine woman, another spell. Without luck, he comforted himself with the knowledge that she was still alive, even if it was not with him. Still, he never forgot Ayhana, much like one never forgets when something is missing or out of place. It's almost as if the remembering meant that she was still there, even as a dream. Even only under the full moon.

And Ayhana's story grew into myth and legend, reminding children not to disturb the forest spirits or trouble cursed waters. Even so, when other foolish village boys inevitably dared each other to swim in the water and drink from the pond, they seemed quite alright afterwards. Some even thought they saw a wolf watch them carefully through the reeds.

When Amadeo finishes, the children sit back in disappointment. They furrow their brows, frustrated at the end of this raw, incomplete story. They wait for Amadeo to reveal the lesson, the reason why he decided to tell them this myth they'd all heard before, at one time or another. Was this a warning not to disobey the forest spirits?

But Amadeo ignores their protests and gets to his feet. He takes a torch from the fire and leaves the children behind without another word. They know better than to follow him.

As the sun succumbs to the darkness, Amadeo follows the path behind his house and through the woods. He breathes in the coming night, feeling the air crispen in his lungs, dew-sweet and alive. He slowly walks up towards the tree at the top of the hill, his soul groaning under the weight of this cumbersome body.

A white-muzzled wolf waits for him at the foot of the tree.

'At last,' he whispers as he holds Ayhana in his arms, feeling her body shift beneath his embrace.

'Hold me, darling,' she whispers hoarsely.

They stay like that, Ayhana and Amadeo, until their eyes hold a new horizon that only they can see.

SARAFINA

Since I was nine, she has been my best friend, accompanying me through my formative years and my hardest moments. Sarafina's unwavering love and presence were there as I grew and changed, loving me in all my forms. Even when she fell ill, our bond remained strong. While everything changed, her love stayed constant.

She loved me her entire life, and I will love her for the rest of mine.

THE BEDROOM

The happiest place on earth. My bedroom. The place to be, the place to laugh, the place to smile, and the place to just breathe.

Taking one step inside the bedroom, my instincts are as they always have been, and my feet carry my heavy body to the shattered mirror. The black frame enhances the black cuts as if they were a part of the mirror all along. The big cracks make red lines on my fingers when I remove one broken piece. One aspect of my life is in my hand. In the broken glass, I see one of my ponytails, reminding myself of a younger me. A part of my childhood where ponytails meant a stress-free and ignorantly naïve life. I sigh, and that memory becomes clear in my mind. My eyes flicker, my hand grips the shard of glass harder, and the year I turned eleven flashes before my eyes:

My parents permitted me to paint the walls any colour I wanted. At that time, I wanted pink, reflecting my obsession with *My Little Pony*. The soft pink, I smile when I think about it. The girl I used to be opening the door, the warmth that swept over my face, like I was being hugged, embraced by the wall, and greeted by the bed. The new paint smell made my head feel groggy, and the power I felt knowing that this was my decision. My colour, the colour that washed away the reality of the day. The smile I had to fake in the outside world – that smile became real when I stepped over the threshold. I could be me, while I lay on the pink and purple bed sheets.

'Ouch,' I drop the glass and, as it falls, the sun catches its reflection and a faint bright light lands on the wall, only for a second.

I press the blood-covered hand to my mouth to stop the small wound from bleeding. The metallic, salty taste has me smiling and rolling my eyes because of the irony. However, the pain from the red cut on my hand brings me back to the present, which is good, I guess. The realness of feeling like an eleven-year-old again has to be the start of a mental breakdown. 'This is ridiculous!' I yell while I step over the blood pool on the floor. The paintbrush is heavy in my hand, and a few drops hit the new carpet. I walk around the room with a new colour in mind. The door catches my eyes, and I look at the numbers and lines drawn on it. There are two numbers there that represent my height and age. My mother would try and write it on the wall, but I would scream at her. My hands shook like I was freezing, and the shaking would not stop until my mom promised me that she would never write on the walls.

Turning around, my feet feel wet through my fuzzy socks. They stick to my feet, soggy, and the wind from the small dirty window makes the floor feel colder now that they are wet. It's like I am standing in a swamp.

My eyes stare at the door that the mirror is facing away from, and I see the wobbly grey pen marks creating the number fourteen. That year I painted the walls a different colour. The pink felt like a different part of my life. The girliness, sweetness, and childhood were gone. While I grew up, so did the room. The white represented a new and fresh start for me – a teenager who was making new friends and a new addition to the family. White like a doctor's coat, something worn by a person who fixes other people and saves lives.

With the white came the green and brown from the flowers my new stepfather gave me. The dark green leaves contrasted with the calm white walls. The room started to feel and smell like the forest, like growth.

Sitting on my bed, the mirror shows me a full-length image of my body. Every day since That Day, I woke up and saw my new reflection, never the old one. Thinking back, I can't even remember if I chose the placement of the mirror or if the decision was taken out of my hands. The mirror hovering over the bed made that furniture a place of judgement. It became a place far more critical than somewhere for sleeping in. This importance followed me through the years. I ate there, did homework there, made plans there, and lived there. A safe place. Now harmful.

Turning my head, a few blonde, curly, out-of-place strands of hair fall in my eyes and make them water. Through the tears, I see the small slashes on the right side of the wall; underneath the window, small whispers flow through. I cannot make out what they say. I don't know if it is in my imagination or if the walls are trying to speak to me.

'I wonder what colour she is going to use today? I am so excited,' squeals the Wall.

'I am thinking pink again,' the Bed answered.

'What? PINK! No, no, no, pink is already painted on me. I can still feel the smothering sweetness,' the Wall's energetic and innocent voice worries the Bed.

'But... but...we... we...' The Bed tried to stutter his point.

'She cannot paint you! Me, this is mine and her decision. So shut your piehole,' the Wall started to hum happily.

'But we were all happier when you were pink,' the Bed sobbed.

The Wall stopped humming and looked at her tired best friend, wishing she could reach out to her person. The person she has watched grow, the person she's been with through all the phases a girl goes through. The girlish phase, the teenage crisis with a new family, the depression phase, and now the last phase. As if the Bed could read the Wall's thoughts, he gave her a little push by creating a hump that gnawed into her thigh and gave her a leg cramp.

Getting up from the soft bed, I am dizzy, my leg aches, and my body is floating within this room. Walking up to the window, I look at the indent beside the scratches, running my hands over them while my mind takes me back to the incident that changed everything. I press my face against the wall like I did when I was sixteen, and I close my eyes. The wall is my strength, the strength I need to look back, and the rock I needed back then.

My fingers dig into the wall, and the white paint flakes get stuck under my fingernails. I close my eyes, and my body feels cold and numb. The cold sweat on my back intensifies his nasty breath. His touch on my arm creates a moist impression from his thick blistered fingers. The closer he forces himself against my body, the more I press mine into the wall. For a moment, I forget the pain, and I am one with the wall. It has rescued my mind from this horrible incident. The reassuring mumbles drown out the violation that is being done to my body.

Opening my eyes, I try to take a few steps away from the bruised wall, but I slide in the wet patch from the red paint that drips from the hard bristles of the brush. The wall catches me again, and I leave behind a distorted red handprint against the white. I almost knocked over the new flowers he bought me, the old ones I tossed in the trash with my ripped-up clothes three years ago. The fresh flowers are prettier, and they have colours; pink and yellow. I laugh at the thought, pretty, innocent like I was.

This room holds so many memories. I smile when I see my reflection in the full-length mirror. It was a gift, an 'I'm sorry' gift. To make me feel better, but all I remember were the bruises on my neck and wrists. The haunting of the past is stuck in that freaking mirror! The cracks I made in it divide the different parts of me that grew up in this room. Some parts are still whole; others are so cracked I can't see the reflection of my body. My body feels sore, and my wrist aches from carrying the paintbrush. The bed looks so comfy now like I could go to sleep and never wake up. I walk back to the bed and lie down. The window beside the bed lets the sunshine in, and it warms the right side of my face. I just need a few minutes of rest; then, I can keep painting the walls red. Just a few minutes of quiet. No more memories, and no more thoughts, just silence.

DEPENDENCY

In need is desperation,
in desperation change,
for to love is to be transformed
and acquiesce to demand.

You chatter to the sky, the walls,
talk of things that no one sees –
apart from me, for I pretend
to share your vision in need.

To love, to sacrifice, to want,
is to carve out pieces of oneself
in order to allow new growth
to be sheltered in the depth.

For every day, I fight for you
so you may fight for me,
while duty, love and need entwine
'til we can hardly breathe.

HAPPY BIRTHDAY!

'Happy birthday!'

The lights are already off. They walk towards me, a cake in hand with burning bright candles. They are singing. Whose idea was it, to implement such eccentric traditions? I have to smile, because it is my birthday. Because they are doing this for me. Yet they have never asked, not once, if it is a *happy* birthday.

There is a familiarity, I find, that birthdays succumb to sadness.

It's a yearly reflection entitled to our shortcomings rather than our achievements. But it would be wrong, wouldn't it, if we phrased it differently? *Happy birthday?*

It would make an inquisitive, melancholy song. No one would sing it. Silence.

I think I would prefer the silence. I do not have to lie to the silence. Instead, the silence knows all of me, unspoken and morphing. Changing. Changing. Changing.

Birthday — the day we have grown by number. Supposedly, we have grown by society too, but still, we have not grown enough. Not as a person, nor to ourselves nor the imposingly rigorous expectations placed upon us. Will we ever grow enough? I wake up on my birthday, and I am not a different person. Have I failed, this succulent change into a wiser, maturer being?

It is funny when you think too much. I ask myself, if I had awoken different, a version of the person the world is catered for, would I have succeeded? And then I think a little more. It does not matter what form I take — I cannot be everything for everyone. I cannot be a daughter for my mother; a sister for my brother; a shoulder for my friend; a flower for the bees; the sun for the flowers; the moon for the sun; the earth for the moon, nor hope for the earth. I cannot. I am one person at one time. Sometimes, I even fail at being a body for my mind, a mind for my body and a soul for myself.

They begin to congratulate me. I have blown the candles.

'Make a wish,' they say. *A wish.*

Whilst my thoughts divulge in battle between wishes and forlorn optimism, I find there is a theme in that: for every person that wishes me a congratulations my loneliness cuts another tether in my heart. I close my eyes and consider, am I to celebrate this isolated passage of time? I do not see time granting me a worthy favour.

The lights are turned back on, and I decide: I will celebrate when time gives me a second to breathe.

The routine is inscrutable. Next, I am to cut the cake, to take a bite from the first piece. Maybe I have grown out of cake. Does that count? Is that change enough? I have never met a child that would turn down cake. There, I am a worthy contender of your game of adulthood.

So, here comes the immense guilt burdened by birthdays. This is what they spring upon us — a bouquet of attention. I can sense that I am being witnessed in a distorting perspective, a shifting expectation, and I cannot help but feel like an imposter within my own skin.

These eyes.

All of these gazes.

Are you looking at me, or are you looking at someone else entirely?

Maybe I was someone eighteen years ago, but today, I am no more than a sketch. They pass me around, like some icebreaker activity on the first day. Add one thing each and it will bring everyone together. Suddenly I have two heads that can fit two brains that can solve anything. I have wings sprouting from my shoulders, an angel they will call me. Do they know demons can fly too? Someone draws me a heart and the person next to them colours it gold. Such a metal fixture is a heavy weight in my chest.

And after they are all done with me, I am barely human anymore.

I will look in the mirror as I remove my finest clothes. I will strip down to the bare minimum that is human and I will not recognise the reflection. I have changed in every person's eyes. Mine too. At least I will be the last person to whisper that message. To finish the cycle of that year. As I am searching in the glassy portrait, for the human inside of me, I will confirm it myself.

Happy birthday.

THE TOOTHBRUSH

'Dry your eyes.'

'I'm not crying,' she replies, matching the forcefulness in his tone.

'You're about to,' he says sharply, placing his hands on his waist and looking bored.

'No, I'm not,' she says with a sharp exhale.

This is what she has learned: *Don't let it affect you, just breathe.*

'Have you got my things?' she asks.

'There.'

He points to the coffee table behind her. Cathy turns and approaches the familiar sitting room. The varnished wood still displays the stains of her coffee mugs and the scratches of the cats' claws. Beneath it, the white plush rug that they'd dry-cleaned because she had spilled red wine, has vanished.

She gazes into the cardboard box of mostly toiletries, all of which lie askew. An amalgamation of years' worth of products, keepsakes, and ornaments. He had obviously packed them quickly and haphazardly. She remembers the time he had told her that she didn't need any of these things to make her look beautiful. But these compliments had been thrown away, much like the objects sitting in this box.

Cathy picks up the box and returns to face him, placing it in front of herself on the shining marble breakfast bar. They had picked it together in expectation of eating breakfast together for the rest of their lives.

'You've changed your hair,' he comments, examining her with his expression.

'Yeah,' she sighs.

She runs a hand through her brown hair, once bleached blonde to within an inch of its life. These days, she seems to have more time to treat herself to simple things like getting her hair done.

'It suits you.'

His words don't matter, she doesn't care enough anymore. She makes no reply but holds his gaze. Looking uncomfortable, he shuffles his weight between his feet and lays his palms flat on the counter. She sighs and looks back to the box of belongings.

'The cat toys are in there as well,' he says as if expecting her to ask.

She shuffles the pots and containers to see the tiny plush toys. The cat will be pleased to see them, Cathy smiles.

'How is he?' He asks with a softer tone.

It makes her stomach churn.

'He's fine. He's a cat. He doesn't know how to miss you.'

Her tone is blunt and hostile because he doesn't deserve her soft tones, not anymore. *Don't let it affect you, just breathe.*

'Yeah, but I'll miss him,' he says, again in that wistful tone.

'I'll mention you to him, but he doesn't have much conversation.'

He looks momentarily shocked that she's made a joke, as if he can't quite believe she could still have a sense of humour.

'Don't be nasty, he was as much a part of this house as you were,' he says candidly.

'Yeah, but it's not *my* fault we're not here anymore.'

She realises that she has managed it. He looks to the ground. With regret? With sorrow? With some form of longing? She can't tell, but she is pleased with herself.

She continues to search through the box, hoping not to return here a second time, she scours it for everything material that has ever mattered to her. The bright blue mug from her twenty-fifth birthday and the glass tankard from Oktoberfest had been wrapped in leaves of newspapers. The same as the small porcelain bulldog that his mother had given her out of a museum from their trip to Amsterdam. A photo album, some hair clips and scrunchies, and abandoned at the bottom of the box, all her jewellery. They had been thrown carelessly, left to cheapen amongst the bobby pins. He had bought her most of it, once upon a time.

'I don't think my face cream is in here?' she says and frowns up at him.

He crosses his arms and tells her to go and look in the bathroom, shooing her away as if she were an irritating fly. He pulls the smoothie shaker in front of him as she leaves.

With a huff, she hurries to the bathroom at the end of the hallway. The tiles and the mirror in the bathroom are covered in condensation, and the room itself is filled with the familiar scent of his Lynx body wash. It would seem sentimental if the smell wasn't so strong.

Cathy's hands press against the porcelain sink and she lowers her head, reprising a position she held six months ago.

Has it really been that long?

She stares at her blurred reflection in the mirror, but it changes and suddenly she remembers the tear-streaked face and the red blotches on the tiled floor, as clear as they had looked in that moment. Then she remembers her hands wrapping around herself and the horrid stings of pain blaring across her abdomen before she had fallen to the floor in agony.

Until this moment, Cathy had missed her house, but now, she felt like a stranger.

She finds her face cream in the small cupboard – the very

cupboard she had kept her pregnancy tests in – and then she notices the counter. In the small marble glass next to the tap are two toothbrushes, but only one of them looks familiar.

With her face cream clenched in her fist, Cathy returns to the kitchen with a frown.

'There's a toothbrush in the bathroom that isn't mine or yours,' she says quickly.

He pauses and stares at her. Around him lie the ingredients for his whey protein shake. He had been drinking them for months now, perhaps that's when he had started to change.

'The toothbrush is a spare,' he says easily with a deep frown.

'No one has spare toothbrushes.'

There was a pause.

'You getting jealous, Cath?' he asks with a grin.

In her head, she believes she's rather thrilled that somebody else has taken him off her hands because she doesn't recognise the man standing in front of her anymore. In fact, looking at him now, she doesn't recognise him as the man she had once loved.

She knows she has changed, grown more confident, felt more invincible, but apart from her hair, she was exactly the same.

His phone chimes and he seems unable to get there quick enough. *It must be her*, Cathy thinks to herself. He puts his phone back in his pocket after replying and turns his attention back to her.

'Is she on her way?' Cathy asks, the blunt boldness to her tone lights a fire in her belly.

'You shouldn't ask questions that you won't like the answer to,' he says with a smirk.

Something he used to say a lot, and always with that same smirk. At least, Cathy thinks, he still has that childish smirk. It is the one thing confirming that she was definitely speaking to him.

Until now, she thought she had been speaking to some strange, transformed being that just so happened to look like him.

'Fine, she stays here, is that what you want to hear – that I've moved on, that someone else has taken your place?'

Cathy licks her lips and shakes her head. 'I was going to say something about respect, but then you never really knew what that meant, did you?' she asks.

He sighs, so audibly that his chest rises. 'I did respect you.'

'Not after that, you didn't,' she says, hoping he understands the message. She can't bring herself to say the words.

'You were grieving something that never existed.'

'It existed to me! That's what you have *never* understood.'

'There was nothing there! *How* many times do we have to go through this!'

His face is red, and his arms fly out from his sides in anger.

Don't let it affect you, just breathe, she thinks to herself.

'You may have kept the house, but you were the one who walked out. It was you who couldn't deal with the grief,' she says and stabs her finger towards him.

He looks defeated. His hands fall to his sides, he appears to calm himself down, but she's never seen him that animated. When he speaks next, his tone turns bored once again.

'Have you got everything now?'

Cathy tilts her head, there is nothing left in his expression that suggests he ever cared, and it no longer upsets her. She picks up the box from the counter and feels her whole body itching to leave the house for the last time.

'Yes, and you can keep the TV, by the way. I've just bought a bigger one.'

DISLOCATES

I'm still waiting,
stationary pacing
while they all watch.
Told I'll wake up
one morning, the penny
will drop.
It never has, it never will,
I'll stay the same standing
still with my head in the clouds.
While everyone stares
from their chairs of airs
and graces.
Told to gracefully grow
into something that shows
I'm a child no more.
But an adult with thoughts
afforded no time to figure
out what I want
from myself.
So, I bend to fit a mould
that dislocates not only me
but my joints,
fractures bones
and draws blood.
All to say I've changed
when the answer really
is
that I only wish I could.

ESTRANGEMENT

HOME

Home. I was not sure of what the word meant anymore. Was it my place of origin? Was it where I felt I belonged? Surely, I could not fit into one place only. The concept seemed universally singular, yet my home was plural. It was multidimensional, happening at the same time in different towns, at different times in the same place. Home was a concept I twisted and turned around my fingers like the hair tie I used when I was anxious, trying to grasp its meaning. Thinking of home was like tearing apart two pieces of my heart I had been trying to sew together for more than a year now.

I grew up in another country, speaking a different language. My culture was a treasure I would forever hold close to my heart. Now, I had to make room for a new one and embrace its various heritages.

The first upheaval in my habits as a child, after my sister's birth, happened in 2005. My parents bought their first apartment, which meant we had to leave the one they were renting. The new one was merely a few streets away though; we stayed in the same town. I finally had my own bedroom, my parents had a small shower room to themselves. Daph was one, I was four. I remember choosing the green wallpaper with little cows, suns and houses adorning my room, and tearing it down eight years later to paint the walls to sell the flat. I did not realise, until now, that while I was doodling on the paper before peeling it off, I was saying goodbye to the innocence of childhood. So, we moved after that, only a couple of streets away. The walls went from green to purple, the new white wardrobe doors welcomed posters, pictures, and souvenirs that evolved throughout my teenage years. More and more music sheets piled up on the desk and spread on the floor. In this flat, I managed to create a little cocoon so that, when it did not feel like home at times, I had a shelter in my room. A few years later came a time when I had no home at all, nowhere to be grounded to. I still came back to the same apartment after a school day. But I was slowly losing against depression, and I did not belong anywhere anymore, not even in my own body. The echoes of the flute got replaced by those of anxiety and despair.

I do not think I have ever been braver than the day I crossed the English Channel on my own, armed with what I had decided was absolutely necessary packed in two suitcases and a pink duffle bag. Tears streaming down my face, I walked through the gates of the Eurostar without looking back at what had just become my old life. I had not yet reached Aberystwyth, the final destination, when I was already struck by culture shock. Public transport. I used to complain a lot about the French railways, so did everyone. After that day, Saturday 24 September 2022, I swore I would never speak ill of it ever again. Incredibly enough, I had managed to find a worse company than the SNCF. Avanti West Coast. After three different trains, a few hours spent standing trying to hold my luggage together, many struggles and a few anxiety tears shed; I dropped my bags on the university accommodation carpet and began unpacking old memories in a new room.

The question 'Where do you come from?' came inherently with meeting a lot of people with diverse nationalities. At the beginning of the year, I would always refer to Paris as home. Then, as new habits started sinking in, in Aberystwyth, I would say things like 'my parents live in Paris' or 'my parents' place is in Paris.' The process of replacing one home with another had begun without much thought, it flowed quite naturally out of my mouth. I had adjusted quite well to a drastically different life.

The Christmas break was a key moment of my relationship to home. I had been homesick for a few weeks before going back. I missed my family, my cat, cheese, bread and wine, café terrasses and gossip with friends. The perfect French cliché I had wanted to avoid slapped me in the face late November. The hardest moments were those spent on the phone with my parents. I was confronted with what I had in Aberystwyth that made me happy, and what I could be having at home – had I not moved abroad. That was when the uncomfortable tearing sensation settled. In my head, being homesick not only meant betraying the life I was finally building for myself, but also failure. The only comfort I found in this longing was that I had not forsaken my culture nor my roots. A duality had started to grow within me, and I had no choice but to embrace it. Then it was time to go back. I travelled to Paris all day long, with no train failure or cancellation to deplore.

After a few weeks spent home, a strange sensation kicked in. Things like adapting my timetable to others; having dinner depending on when my mother would come back for work; constant background noises like the tv or my dad and sister arguing, would sometimes be overwhelming. I felt like while I had matured abroad, time had stood still in Paris, and I had outgrown it. I found myself longing for the autonomy I had developed on my own. I could not put my finger on precise words to describe how I felt, I hated that. Eventually, I managed to find it. I could not be homesick, because I was home. So instead, I was Aberysick. I missed the life I had created for myself overseas. Making this word up helped me feel comfortable with the notion of having two different places weighing the same in my heart.

When getting to know new people over the year, I have had conversations with some who did not understand why I chose to move to Aberystwyth to go to university, once they knew I came from Paris.

'You have everything you need there, why did you end up in the middle of nowhere in Wales?'

'You lived in Paris and you came here?'

Somehow, they did not understand why I would have moved from the glamourous city of lights to a small Welsh town. What they did not get is that this was one of the exact reasons I fled. I often replied that when you lived there, you either loved it or bore it as a burden, and that in my case, that burden had become too heavy for me to carry, so I shook it off my shoulders and left. That here, in Aberystwyth, I felt closer to nature, more grounded, more at peace. The air I breathed was purer, the sounds that woke me up in the morning were not cars and roadworks anymore, but seagulls. That here, I felt like I was starting to understand who I was, after having searched for it for years, stuck between the four walls of depression imprisoning my mind. Surrounded by endless fields, green hills and the sea, I felt like I was finally understanding the difference between surviving and living. It was like I had constantly been struggling to keep my head out of the water before, whereas I could finally float on the back and follow the tides without them swamping me. Aberystwyth was that place I had been looking for where I could greet myself and get rid of the past that had been following me like a clingy shadow, displaying 'depressed' on my forehead. Moving there was the fresh start I needed to understand what it meant to enjoy my own company and get rid of the constant fog of negativity.

The other day, I read something that said 'home is where you have your people at.' I pondered on this, and realised I strongly disagreed. The people I loved were in two countries and came into my life at different times. I carried them in my heart and kept them in mind no matter where I was. I believed that, instead, home was where I found myself and fell in love with me.

ON A DAY LIKE THIS

you sit at the seam
where the shore meets the sea
and shake the absence of
him
      from your trainers like grit, the stubborn silt
      washed clean by the cerulean water.

      Your first best friend
      had blue eyes, green at the retina,
like a
    rockpool.
    Go
    wading; listen
to the harbour singing like your mother
      after a long work week - the steam
      from her coffee curling around her
          like jet fuel.

      Recall the slow worm,
supine in your hands like a shard of
the moon.

Let the memory
      thrash, a fish in a net; your future stretching out against a
      radium sunset;
          skin stretched thin over
cartilage.

Swim out to it.

Shuck oysters

with your teeth like wild fruit.

Spit the pip.

     Grow a forest.

We asked visitors and participants at the 2024 Refugee Week Celebration (organised as part of Imaginary Homelands) in Aberystwyth to draw or write whatever they wanted on a piece of paper. This is the result:

ACKNOWLEDGEMENTS

Our MA anthology is proudly supported by funding from the 'Imaginary Homelands' project, a collaborative initiative with the Centre for Creative Wellbeing. This funding is part of a two-year agreement with Broken Sleep Books to publish the Creative Writing MA Anthology, a central feature of the Writer as Professional Module in the ECW department. This initiative allows our students to immerse themselves in the creation, design, and editing of an anthology that not only showcases their exceptional creative and critical work but also grants them their first publication opportunity.

Managed entirely by Creative Writing MA students, the anthology's theme explores concepts of home, displacement, change, place, and identity. For many students, this may be their first opportunity to become published writers.

For more details about the Imaginary Homelands project, please contact Dr Naji Bakhti at anb106@aber.ac.uk.

ROBIN LUFFMAN — EDITOR-IN-CHIEF

Robin is a lover of speculative fiction, particularly folklore. They write mainly about their home county of Derbyshire, using the many odd and unusual goings-on there to explore class, gender, and deeply strange people.

ALISON EHRINGER — POETRY AND PROSE EDITOR

Alison is a reader, writer, and oat milk enthusiast who specialises in gender and queer studies in a historical context. She has a particular interest in speculative fiction and likes experimenting with temporal and spatial distance through unnatural narratives.

BLUE STARENG — MARKETING

Blue is a writer and reader of dark erotic fiction and psychological thrillers. Her past experiences and mental health journey have influenced her writing since she was younger. Recently, she has begun implementing the most important thing into her writing... music.

LAURA JANOSIK — PROSE EDITOR

Laura's interest spans from gothic literature and folkloric fantasy to soft science-fiction. She loves writing character-driven stories that feel like a comforting hug before she stabs her readers in the back with a heart-wrenching moment.

LARA SCHAELE — MARKETING

Lara is an avid reader and writer of psychological realism with a special fondness for contemporary romances. She loves happy endings and books that make her cry and will always put a piece of her real life into her writing.

LOUISE ROWLAND — ART AND POETRY EDITOR

Louise is a writer of all things supernatural with a particular interest in gothic fiction. Her writing explores realism with the occasional ghost or vampire causing chaos. She loves classic fiction the most and can talk for hours about Shakespeare's plays.

KLAV MORRIS — MARKETING

Klav is best described as a "creative nightmare." If they aren't writing, they're drawing or crocheting or picking up yet another hobby. They vary between writing supernatural and folklore-inspired stories to writing YA and romance, and read anything that isn't nailed down.

LAY OUT YOUR UNREST

www.ingramcontent.com/pod-product-compliance
Lightning Source LLC
Chambersburg PA
CBHW030848090426
42737CB00009B/1142